PREPPER PETE's GUN for A SON

Written by Kermit Jones, Jr.
Illustrated by Christy Brill

To James, for answering countless questions,
and to my great-Uncle Farley for my first gun.
– K.E.J.J.

Visit
www.PrepperPeteAndFriends.com/GunSafety
to learn more!

IMPORTANT: This book is only to be used as a launching point of discussion with children.
It is not intended to be a substitute for an actual firearms safety course.
The author assumes no liability. It is recommended that you seek out a local safety course in
your area and attend with your child to demonstrate the importance of gun safety.

Text copyright ©2014 by Kermit E. Jones, Jr.
Illustrations copyright ©2014 by Christy Brill
Cover design and digital layout by Jeff Eskridge
All rights reserved. Published by Kamel Press, LLC.

Library of Congress Control Number: 2014904826

978-1-62487-020-0 Paperback
978-1-62487-022-4 Hardcover
978-1-62487-023-1 eBook

Published in the USA

There once was an ant named Prepper Pete.

When his son, Charlie, became old enough, Pete bought Charlie a gun.

As a Prepper and responsible citizen,
Pete knew the importance of gun safety.

He taught Charlie that even though
there are many toy guns,
a real gun is not a toy.

A gun can be very dangerous if not
handled properly, so Pete and Charlie
enrolled in a gun safety class together.

To help them remember gun safety,
they learned the phrase,
"Treat, Never, Keep, Keep."

The first rule is,
"**TREAT** every gun as if it is loaded."

Rule two is, "**NEVER** allow the muzzle to point at something you don't intend to shoot or destroy."

The muzzle is the end of the barrel. Good muzzle control means always keeping the gun pointed in a safe direction.

Rule three is, "**KEEP** the gun safety on until you are ready to shoot."

This means the gun should already be pointing at the target when you turn the safety off.

The fourth rule is, "**KEEP** your finger off the trigger until you are ready to shoot."

A straight finger on the side of the trigger guard is called a good trigger finger.

Prepper Pete and Charlie were also taught to "**CHECK** to make sure the chamber is empty before handing a gun to someone else."

The chamber is the place where the bullet goes.

"**NEVER** look down the barrel of a gun or point it at another person."

They also learned the importance of
personal safety equipment.
Always wear your "eyes and ears"
(safety goggles and hearing protection).

They were taught that

bullets can travel a very long way, so…

"**ALWAYS** be sure of your target
and what is behind and beyond it."

17

"DON'T RUSH!"

When people rush, accidents can happen.

Remember the motto,
"Slow is smooth, and smooth is fast."

Take your time and be careful.
This will usually be faster and safer than
rushing and making a mistake.

During the class, Charlie and his father learned the meaning of **BRASS**.

- **BREATHE**
- **RELAX**
- **AIM**
- **SQUEEZE**
- **SHOOT**

BREATH.

You should always breath
slow and steady.

RELAX.

Stay calm and
do not get excited or nervous.

AIM carefully.

Remember to keep your finger off the trigger
until you are "sighted in" to your target.

SQUEEZE.

Squeeze the trigger gently...
don't pull or jerk it fast.

SHOOT.

If you are squeezing correctly, the gun
should surprise you a little when it fires.
Remember to keep handling it safely!

"**BE SAFE**, and always store guns SAFEly."

They should be stored unloaded in a safe…

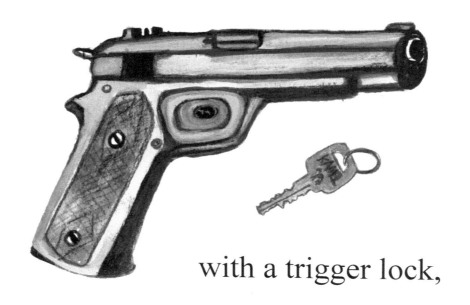

with a trigger lock,

or with a breech cable.

"NEVER TOUCH a gun that you find, and never let other children touch it."

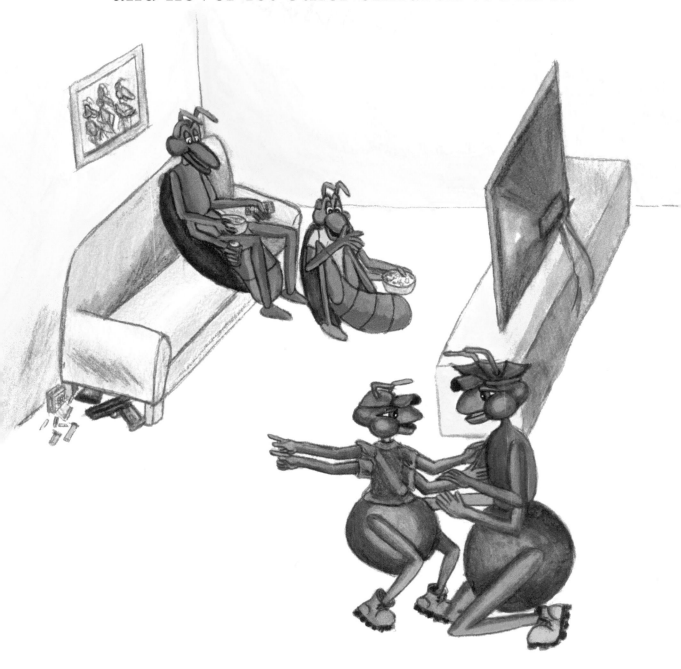

Instead, go get an adult immediately.

If your friend wants to show you a gun,
ask their parents for help.
Never go looking for a gun without an adult!

Charlie learned that gun safety is *everyone's* responsibility. He even signed a contract and promised to follow all gun safety rules.

Gun Safety Contract

To Mom and Dad:

I Promise:

- I will not touch a gun without permission.

- I will never play with guns.

- If I find a gun, I will not touch it; I will tell an adult immediately.

- I will obey all gun safety rules.

Signed: *Charlie*

Visit
www.PrepperPeteAndFriends.com/GunSafety
to print and sign this contract.

A NOTE FOR KIDS!

Ask a grownup to help you print and sign the "Gun Safety Contract" like the one Charlie and his dad, Prepper Pete, signed.

There are many toy guns out there, but remember that real guns are not toys! Guns can be very dangerous if you are not careful.

Even airsoft and BB guns can be dangerous and you should follow safety rules!

Remember that "good practice makes good habits" and you should always practice safety!

KEEP PREPPING!

GUN SAFETY RULES

1) TREAT every gun as if it is loaded.

2) NEVER allow the muzzle to point at something you don't
   intend to shoot, hurt, and destroy.

3) KEEP the gun safety on until you are ready to shoot.

4) KEEP your finger off the trigger until you are ready to shoot.

5) ALWAYS be sure of your target and what is behind it.

6) CHECK to make sure the chamber is empty before handing a
   gun to someone else.

7) NEVER look down the barrel of a gun and never point a gun
   at another person.

8) NEVER TOUCH a gun that you find or let other children
   touch it. Go tell an adult immediately.

9) BE SAFE. Store guns safely & wear your "eyes & ears."

10) DON'T RUSH! Slow is smooth; smooth is fast.

11) BRASS - Breath, Relax, Aim, Squeeze, Shoot.

A NOTE FOR GROWNUPS

If knowledge is power, then in the case of firearms, "knowledge is safety."

Familiarity with guns for kids often helps avoid the "forbidden fruit" syndrome, which can create a safer environment. When they are an appropriate age, work with your kids to familiarize them with firearms, and always stress the importance of gun safety!

IMPORTANT: This book is intended to be used as a launching point of discussion with children. It is **not** intended to be a substitute for an actual firearms safety course.

Seek out a local safety course in your area, and attend with your child to demonstrate to them the importance of gun safety.

Visit
www.PrepperPeteAndFriends.com/GunSafety
for more resources.

LOOK FOR THESE OTHER BOOKS ABOUT PREPPER PETE & FRIENDS!

PREPPER PETE PREPARES
There are many reasons to prepare! Join our favorite Prepper as he introduces kids to some of them!

PREPPER PETE'S "BE PREPARED!
Is your family ready? Join our favorite Prepper as he helps kids understand what they can do to be better prepared for emergencies they might face!

SURVIVALIST SAM STOCKS UP
Learn about the importance of Beans, Bullets, Bandages, and Bad Guys with Prepper Pete's best friend.

PREPPER PETE GETS OUT OF DODGE
When the time comes to leave town, our hero grabs his family and takes them to safety using OPSEC (Operational Security) along the way.

Visit
www.PrepperPeteAndFriends.com
for more!

ABOUT THE AUTHOR

Kermit Jones, Jr. stumbled across the idea of a prepper book for kids when trying to decide how to explain the topic to his four young daughters. Having grown up in a rural setting, he went on to graduate from the U.S. Naval Academy and serve for over a decade on Active Duty, first as a Surface Warfare Officer and later as a Navy Chaplain. Between his kids and his career, he has learned that it's important to always "be prepared!"

ABOUT THE ILLUSTRATOR

Christy Alexander Brill is a native of Wilmington, NC. Proudly married to a United States Marine, and the mother of three young children, she understands the importance of being prepared.

CPSIA information can be obtained
at www.ICGtesting.com
Printed in the USA
LVHW050009081020
668276LV00002B/50